This
BLOOMSBURY Activity Book
belongs to:

D0494102

BLOOMSBURY
Activity Books

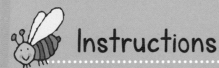

Instructions

Tear out the pages and follow the instructions to create your very own fascinatingly fun fold-up facts. Some of the fold-ups are already completed so you can find out incredible facts about wildlife. Others are packed full of questions for you to answer that will test your wildlife knowledge. And some have been left blank so you can write your own facts!

How to make your fold-up:

 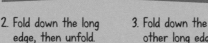 

1. Tear out the page.

2. Fold down the long edge, then unfold.

3. Fold down the other long edge.

4. Unfold, then turn over.

5. Fold the corners in so they meet in the middle.

6. Turn the square over so that the text faces upwards.

7. Fold the corners in again so they meet in the middle.

8. Fold the square in half to form a rectangle.

9. Pinch the corners together and squeeze inwards until they meet.

10. Turn your fold-up upside down and place your thumb and forefinger in each flap.

How to use your fold-up

1. Ask a friend to choose an animal or colour from the four options on your fold-up.
2. Spell out the letters of their choice by moving your fingers for each letter.
3. When you reach the final letter, show your friend the inside of your fold-up and ask them to choose one of the images inside.
4. Count the number of objects in the image by moving your fingers, as before.
5. When you finish, ask them to choose an image again.
6. Lift the flap to reveal the random fact underneath!
7. Close your fold-up, pick another animal and play again!

These fold-ups have been completed for you. Get ready to tear, fold and find out exciting facts about different animals and plants!

Did you know?
Squirrels alert each other to danger by twitching their tails. They would make excellent spies!

Did you know?
Badgers will not poo in their sett; instead they create a special area where they go to the loo.

Did you know?
A hedgehog has about 5,000 spines on its back. You wouldn't want to tread on one by accident – ouch!

Did you know?
A rabbit can jump distances up to one metre – that's a big distance for little legs!

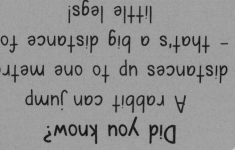

Did you know?
Foxes hide leftover food
so they can come back
and munch on it later.
A midnight feast
in the wild!

Did you know?
Frogs spend the summer
eating as much as they can.
This is so they can reserve
some food for the colder
months to come.

Did you know?
Roe deer like to nibble on
tasty leaves. They've been
known to creep into gardens
at night to gobble
up plants!

Did you know?
A hedgehog's whiskers are
very important – they use
them to track down slugs
and worms to eat.

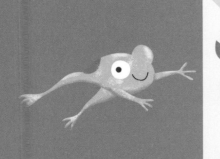

Did you know?
Red foxes are super speedy and can run at speeds of nearly 30 miles per hour!

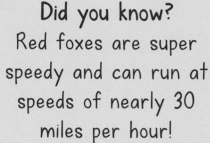

Did you know?
Moles are very fast diggers. In one hour they can dig an underground tunnel over four metres long.

Did you know?
Brown hares can run at speeds of nearly 45 miles per hour!

Did you know?
Mice may be tiny, but they can run as fast as adults. They can only keep up this speed for short distances though.

Did you know?
Bees can extract the
nectar from bluebells
without pollinating
the flower.

Did you know?
The waxy coating
around a tree's
trunk helps it to
conserve water.

Did you know?
You can eat the leaves
and flowers of wild
garlic. They taste really
good cooked in soups
and stews!

Did you know?
The cuckooflower is
one of the orange-
tip caterpillar's
favourite foods.

Did you know?
Primroses have two different types of flower. One type is called 'pin-eyed' and one type is called 'thrum-eyed'.

Did you know?
The branches of a fir tree grow in a whorl around the trunk each year. You can tell how old a tree is by counting the rings inside its trunk.

Did you know?
When poppies start to grow in the fields it means the ground is ready for crops to be planted.

Did you know?
Sunflowers can grow as tall as trees. The tallest sunflower ever recorded was nearly 10 metres tall!

Did you know?
The beautiful patterns on a peacock butterfly's wings are called 'eyes'. They aren't real eyes though!

Did you know?
Ladybirds are pretty to look at, but watch out as they sometimes squirt smelly liquid from their legs!

Did you know?
Bumblebees are garden superheroes. They carry pollen from plant to plant which helps fruit, vegetables and other plants to grow.

Did you know?
Caterpillars turn into beautiful butterflies and moths. You can tell what type of butterfly or moth they will be by looking at their colour.

Did you know?
Dragonflies have bulging, big, round eyes – all the better to spot tasty bugs to eat!

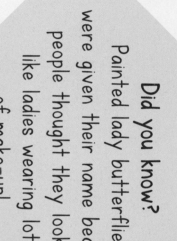

Did you know?
Painted lady butterflies were given their name because people thought they looked like ladies wearing lots of make-up!

Did you know?
When a caterpillar hatches it eats its way out of its eggshell. This helps it to grow big and strong.

Did you know?
Earthworms are one of the only animals that are male and female at the same time!

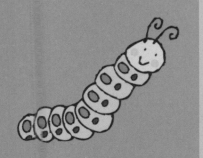

Did you know?
Baby swans are called cygnets. They have grey or brown feathers. Some people mistake cygnets for ugly ducklings!

Did you know?
When herring gulls drink seawater they extract the salt using special glands on their eyes so they don't get dehydrated. Clever!

Did you know?
Puffins love to eat fish. When they spot a tasty fish swimming in the water, they dive in and catch it in their beak.

Did you know?
Male mallards make low quacking sounds – they leave most of the loud talking to the females!

Did you know?
Herons use their toes
to brush their feathers.
Well, they can't pick up
a comb with their
wings can they?

Did you know?
You can spot the
difference between a
female and a male kingfisher
by looking at their beaks.
Females' beaks have
an orange
flash.

Did you know?
Feral pigeons often live
in big cities. They are in the
same family as doves,
which are symbols
of hope.

Did you know?
Magpies do not migrate in
the winter. It is rare for a
magpie to travel more than
10 kilometres from where
it was hatched.

These fold-ups are only half-completed. You need to find the answers to the questions in order to finish them. You can find the answers at the end of the section.

1

Which bird can
turn its head
270 degrees?

2

Which bird puffs
up its red chest in
winter to keep warm?

3

What is the
largest group of birds
that can fly?

4

Can you
think of some
different ways that birds
might 'glue' their nests together?

Why don't you often hear great spotted woodpeckers singing?

_____

_____

_____

Turtle doves feature in one of the most famous Christmas songs of all time. Can you name it?

During mating season, male blue tits do their best to win over the females. How do you think they do this?

Can you name a song about blackbirds?

9

Geese can live in lots of different wild habitats, but where are you most likely to spot them?

What colour are a sparrow's feathers?

12

What does a moorhen look like?

10

Can you name a beautiful blue and orange bird?

11

13
These tiny mammals are known for hanging upside down and coming out at night. Can you name them?

14
Have you ever heard a hedgehog creeping around your garden at night? What sound did it make?

15
These tiny little specks swim around in ponds and rivers. They grow up and turn into frogs. What are they called?

16
Female rabbits are called does. Can you find out what male rabbits are called?

17
Red squirrels
have more fingers
than they do toes.
How many fingers do you
think they have?

20
Rabbits can
stamp, jump and
run really fast. What is
the most powerful part of
a rabbit's body?

18
Baby badgers
have the same
name as baby lions.
What are they called?

19
Mice can
squeeze through
the tiniest of spaces.
How do they decide if they
can fit through a space?

21

Only one gender of the orange-tip butterfly actually has orange on their wings. Is it the males or the females?

- - - - - - - - - - - - - - -

What do spiders use their web for?

24

Where can you find a snail's eyes?

22

How many sets of wings does a black beetle have?

23

25

Why do slugs leave a trail of slime behind them?

26

Cardinal spiders can grow to a really big size. Can you guess how long their legs can grow?

27

What is the name for the creature that hatches from a fly's egg?

28

What happens to honey bees when they release their sting on a human?

29
Sunflowers
feature in one of
the world's most famous
paintings. Can you name
the artist who painted it?

Some trees
grow delicious fruit
for us to eat. Can you
name a fruit that grows on trees?

30

A pretty pink
garden flower shares
part of its name with the
fox. Can you name it?

31

32
What colour
are the flowers
of a forget-me-not?

33
Star-shaped water lilies float on ponds and lakes. In stories they are the perfect resting place for which small animal?

34
Snowdrops are delicate small white flowers. Where do they grow?

35
Daisies make beautiful necklaces and bracelets. How many daisies can you thread into a daisy chain?

36
Why do children blow on the heads of dandelions?

ANSWERS

1. Owl.
2. Robin.
3. Swans.
4. They use a range of materials, including: spiders' webs, and even their own spit!

5. Because they drum on trees to communicate instead.
6. 12 days of Christmas.
7. Sing-a-song-of-sixpence.
8. Usually, a male blue tit will sing to his lover. Females also choose mates based on how blue his feathers are.

9. They are water birds – you can find them by ponds, lakes and rivers.
10. They have black, brown and white feathers and red and yellow on their beaks.
11. Kingfisher.
12. Brown, black, white and grey.

13. Bats.
14. They 'chirp', which sounds a bit like squeaking. They also snuffle and gobble things.
15. Tadpoles.
16. Buck.

17. Four on each hand.
18. Cubs.
19. They use their whiskers.
20. Its hind legs.

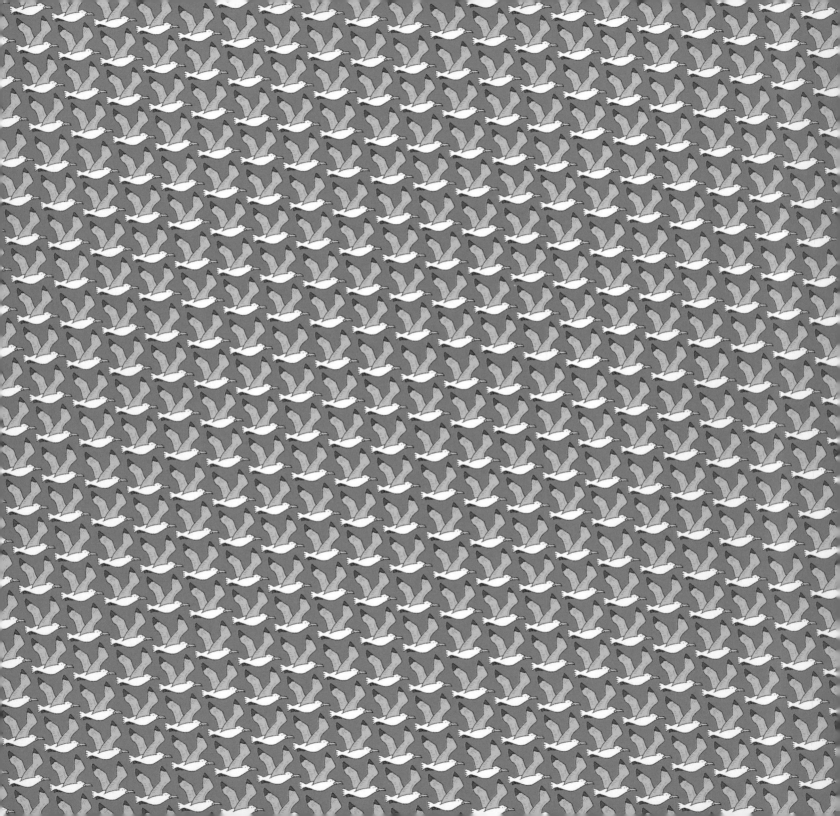

ANSWERS

21. Male.
22. At the end of its feelers.
23. Two.
24. To catch food.

25. So they can find their way home.
26. Up to 14 centimetres.
27. Maggot.
28. They die.

29. Vincent Van Gogh.
30. Pears, apples, plums, oranges, lemons, limes, peaches, figs, papayas, mangoes, cherries, apricots, pomegranates, nectarines, grapefruit just to name a few!
31. Foxgloves.
32. Blue and white, with yellow seeds.

33. Frog.
34. They usually grow in damp woods and forests.
35. Write your own answer.
36. Because they believe that they can tell the time by counting how many heads lift off the stem.

The fold-ups on the next pages have been left blank.
Use this space to write your own amazing facts
about your favourite wildlife.

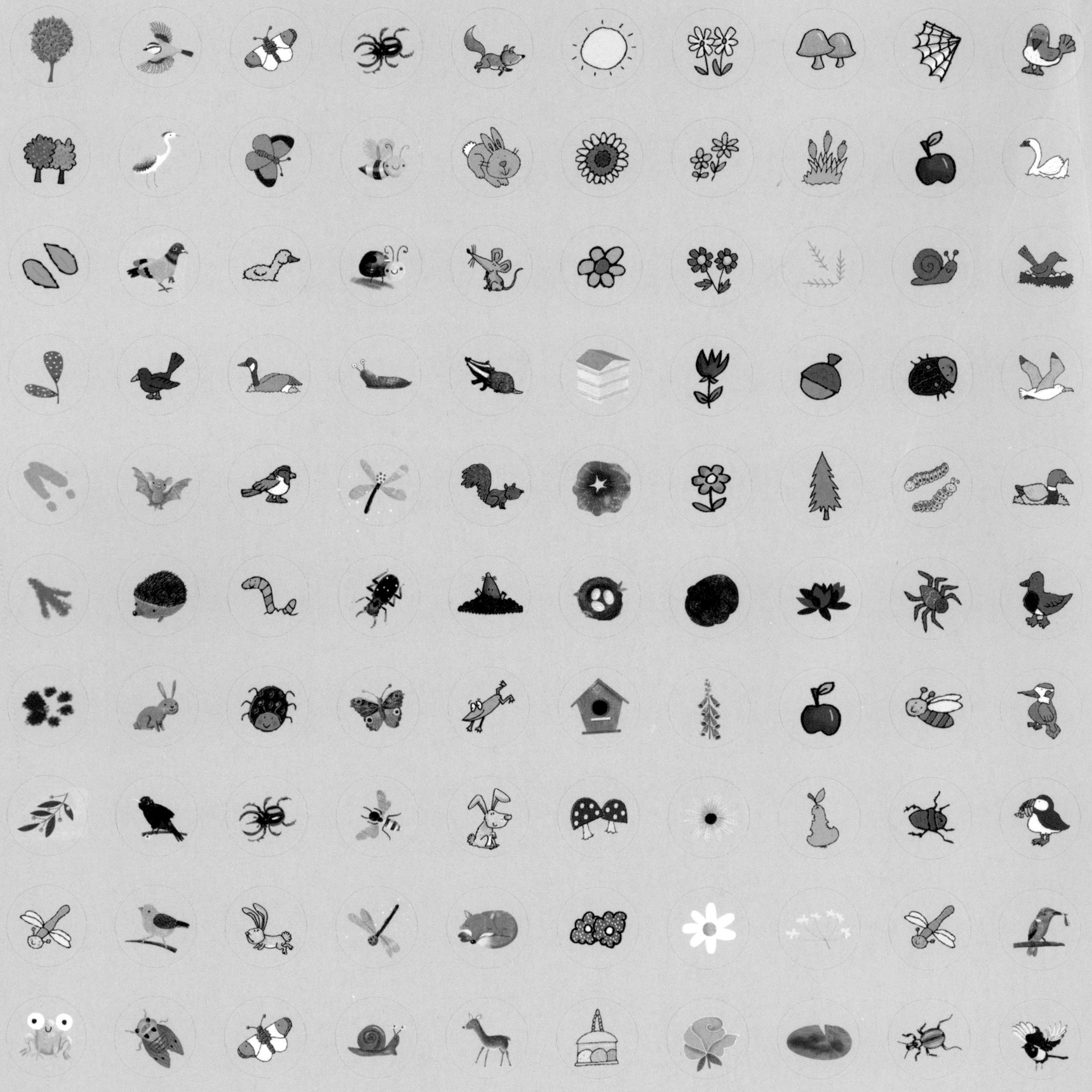

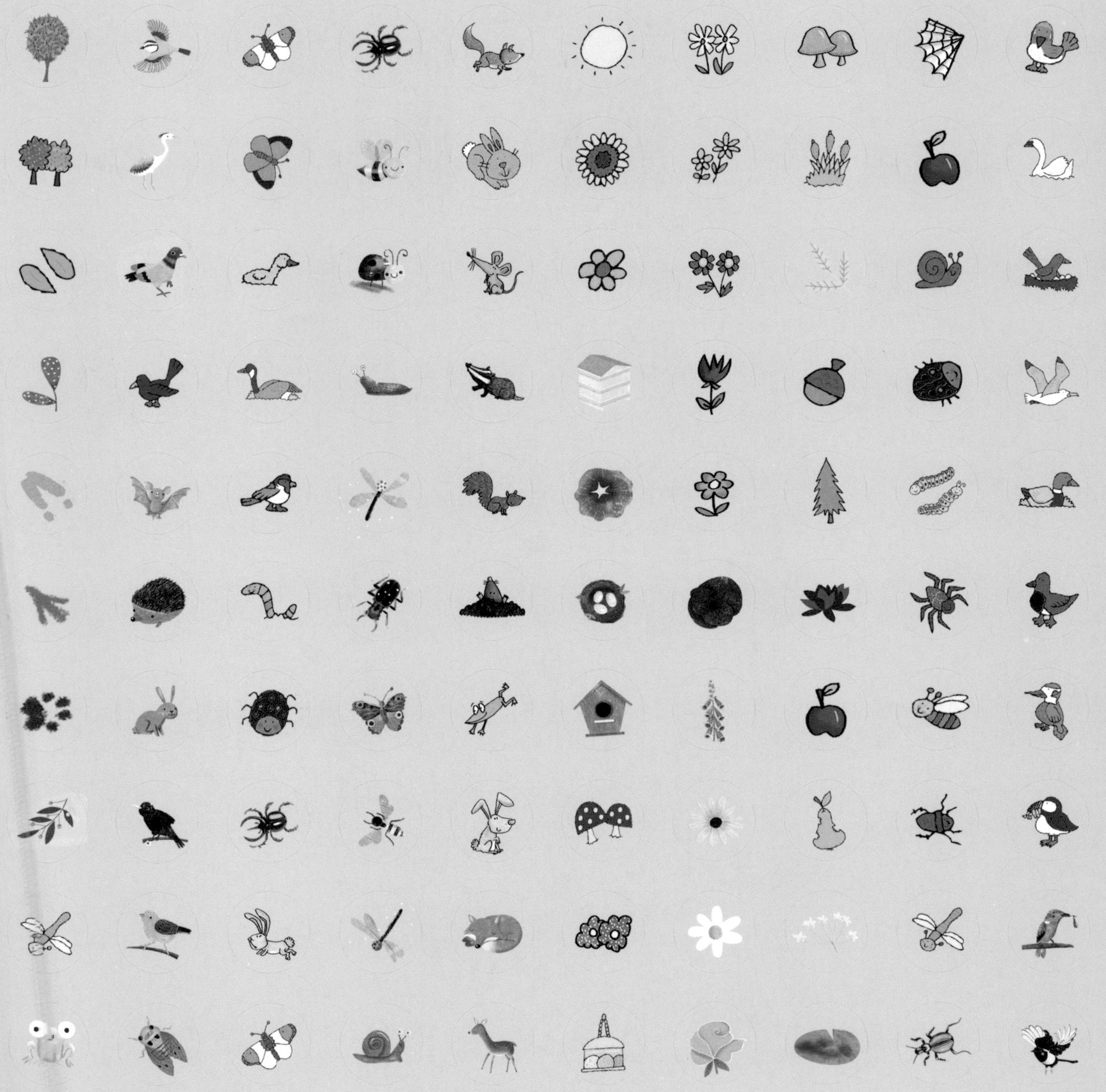